WHEN WE WERE VERY YOUNG

Christine J. Morrison
2 BOYD TERRACE
UIG
ISSE-OP-SKYE

20/2/01

A. A. MILNE

WHEN WE WERE VERY YOUNG

With Decorations by
ERNEST H. SHEPARD

METHUEN CHILDREN'S BOOKS

Also available in paperback

Winnie-the-Pooh
The House at Pooh Corner
Now We Are Six

First published in Great Britain 6th November 1924
by Methuen & Co Ltd
Text by A.A.Milne and illustrations by Ernest H. Shepard
Copyright under the Berne Convention

Coloured edition first published 1989
by Methuen Children's Books
Colouring of the illustrations by Mark Burgess
Copyright © 1989 Methuen Children's Books

Paperback edition first published by Mammoth 1992
Reprinted 1998 by Methuen Children's Books
an imprint of Egmont Children's Books Limited
239 Kensington High Street, London W8 6SA

9 10 8

ISBN 0 7497 1180 9

A CIP catalogue record for this title
is available at the British Library

Printed in Hong Kong

JUST BEFORE WE BEGIN

At one time (but I have changed my mind now) I thought I was going to write a little Note at the top of each of these poems, in the manner of Mr William Wordsworth, who liked to tell his readers where he was staying, and which of his friends he was walking with, and what he was thinking about, when the idea of writing his poem came to him. You will find some lines about a swan here, if you get as far as that, and I should have explained to you in the Note that Christopher Robin, who feeds this swan in the mornings, has given him the name of "Pooh". This is a very fine name for a swan, because, if you call him and he doesn't come (which is a thing swans are good at), then you can pretend that you were just saying "Pooh!" to show how little you wanted him. Well, I should have told you that there are six cows who come down to Pooh's lake every afternoon to drink, and of course they say "Moo" as they come. So I thought to myself one fine day, walking with my friend Christopher Robin, "Moo rhymes with Pooh! Surely there is a bit of poetry to be got out of that?" Well, then, I began to think about the swan on his lake; and at first I thought how lucky it was that his name was Pooh; and then I didn't think about that any more . . . and the poem came quite differently from what I intended . . . and all I can say for it now is that, if it hadn't been for Christopher Robin, I shouldn't have written it; which, indeed, is all I can say for any of the others. So this is why these verses go about together, because they are all friends of Christopher Robin; and if I left out one because it was not quite like the one before, then I should have to leave out the one before because it was not quite like the next, which would be disappointing for them.

Then there is another thing. You may wonder sometimes who is supposed to be saying the verses. Is it the Author, that strange but uninteresting person, or is it Christopher Robin, or some other boy or girl, or Nurse, or Hoo? If I had followed Mr Wordsworth's plan, I could have explained this each time; as it is, you will have to decide for yourselves. If you are not quite sure, then it is probably Hoo. I don't know if you have ever met Hoo, but he is one of those curious children who look four on Monday, and eight on Tuesday, and are really twenty-eight on Saturday; and you never know whether it is the day when he can pronounce his "r's". He had a great deal to do with these verses. In fact, you might almost say that this book is entirely the unaided work of Christopher Robin, Hoo, and Mr Shepard, who drew the pictures. They have said "Thank you" politely to each other several times, and now they say it to you for taking them into your house. "Thank you so much for asking us. We've come."

A.A.M.

CONTENTS

"Vespers," being in the library of the Queen's Dolls'
House, is printed here by special permission.

CORNER-OF-THE-STREET

Down by the corner of the street,
  Where the three roads meet,
    And the feet
Of the people as they pass go "Tweet-tweet-tweet",
Who comes tripping round the corner of the street?
  One pair of shoes which are Nurse's;
  One pair of slippers which are Percy's . . .
    Tweet! Tweet! Tweet!

BUCKINGHAM PALACE

They're changing guard at Buckingham Palace –
Christopher Robin went down with Alice.
Alice is marrying one of the guard.
"A soldier's life is terrible hard,"
                                        Says Alice.

They're changing guard at Buckingham Palace –
Christopher Robin went down with Alice.
We saw a guard in a sentry-box.
"One of the sergeants looks after their socks,"
                                        Says Alice.

They're changing guard at Buckingham Palace –
Christopher Robin went down with Alice.
We looked for the King, but he never came.
"Well, God take care of him, all the same,"
                                        Says Alice.

They're changing guard at Buckingham Palace –
Christopher Robin went down with Alice.
They've great big parties inside the grounds.
"I wouldn't be King for a hundred pounds,"
Says Alice.

They're changing guard at Buckingham Palace –
Christopher Robin went down with Alice.
A face looked out, but it wasn't the King's.
"He's much too busy a-signing things,"
Says Alice.

They're changing guard at Buckingham Palace –
Christopher Robin went down with Alice.
"Do you think the King knows all about *me*?"
"Sure to, dear, but it's time for tea,"
Says Alice.

HAPPINESS

John had
Great Big
Waterproof
Boots on;
John had a
Great Big
Waterproof
Hat;
John had a
Great Big
Waterproof
Mackintosh –
And that
(Said John)
Is
That.

THE CHRISTENING

What shall I call
   My dear little dormouse?
His eyes are small,
   But his tail is e-nor-mouse.

I sometimes call him Terrible John,
'Cos his tail goes on –
And on –
And on.
And I sometimes call him Terrible Jack,
'Cos his tail goes on to the end of his back.
And I sometimes call him Terrible James,
'Cos he says he likes me calling him names. . . .

But I think I shall call him Jim,
   'Cos I *am* fond of him.

PUPPY AND I

I met a Man as I went walking;
We got talking,
Man and I.
"Where are you going to, Man?" I said
   (I said to the Man as he went by).
"Down to the village, to get some bread.
   Will you come with me?" "No, not I."

I met a Horse as I went walking;
We got talking,
Horse and I.
"Where are you going to, Horse, to-day?"
   (I said to the Horse as he went by).
"Down to the village to get some hay.
   Will you come with me?" "No, not I."

I met a Woman as I went walking;
We got talking,
Woman and I.
"Where are you going to, Woman, so early?"
   (I said to the Woman as she went by).
"Down to the village to get some barley.
   Will you come with me?" "No, not I."

I met some Rabbits as I went walking;
We got talking,
Rabbits and I.
"Where are you going in your brown fur coats?"
   (I said to the Rabbits as they went by).
"Down to the village to get some oats.
   Will you come with us?" "No, not I."

I met a puppy as I went walking;
We got talking,
Puppy and I.
"Where are you going this nice fine day?"
  (I said to the Puppy as he went by).
"Up in the hills to roll and play."
"*I'll* come with you, Puppy," said I.

TWINKLETOES

When the sun
Shines through the leaves of the apple-tree,
When the sun
Makes shadows of the leaves of the apple-tree,
Then I pass
On the grass
From one leaf to another
From one leaf to its brother
Tip-toe, tip-toe!
Here I go!

THE FOUR FRIENDS

Ernest was an elephant, a great big fellow,
   Leonard was a lion with a six-foot tail,
George was a goat, and his beard was yellow,
     And James was a very small snail.

Leonard had a stall, and a great big strong one,
   Ernest had a manger, and its walls were thick,
George found a pen, but I think it was the wrong one,
     And James sat down on a brick.

Ernest started trumpeting, and cracked his manger,
   Leonard started roaring, and shivered his stall,
James gave the huffle of a snail in danger
      And nobody heard him at all.

Ernest started trumpeting and raised such a rumpus,
   Leonard started roaring and trying to kick,
James went a journey with the goat's new compass
      And he reached the end of his brick.

Ernest was an elephant and very well-intentioned,
   Leonard was a lion with a brave new tail,
George was a goat, as I think I have mentioned,
      But James was only a snail.

LINES AND SQUARES

Whenever I walk in a London street,
I'm ever so careful to watch my feet;
   And I keep in the squares,
   And the masses of bears,
Who wait at the corners all ready to eat
The sillies who tread on the lines of the street,
   Go back to their lairs,
   And I say to them, "Bears,
Just look how I'm walking in all the squares!"

And the little bears growl to each other, "He's mine,
As soon as he's silly and steps on a line."
And some of the bigger bears try to pretend
That they came round the corner to look for a friend;
And they try to pretend that nobody cares
Whether you walk on the lines or squares.
But only the sillies believe their talk;
It's ever so portant how you walk.
And it's ever so jolly to call out, "Bears,
Just watch me walking in all the squares!"

BROWNIE

In a corner of the bedroom is a great big curtain,
    Someone lives behind it, but I don't know who;
I think it is a Brownie, but I'm not quite certain.
    (Nanny isn't certain, too.)

I looked behind the curtain, but he went so quickly –
    Brownies never wait to say, "How do you do?"
They wriggle off at once because they're all so tickly
    (Nanny says they're tickly too.)

INDEPENDENCE

I never did, I never did, I never *did* like "Now take care,
dear!"
I never did, I never did, I never *did* want "Hold-my-
hand";
I never did, I never did, I never *did* think much of "Not
up there, dear!"
It's no good saying it. They don't understand.

NURSERY CHAIRS

One of the chairs is South America,
One of the chairs is a ship at sea,
One is a cage for a great big lion,
And one is a chair for Me.

The First Chair

When I go up the Amazon,
I stop at night and fire a gun
  To call my faithful band.
And Indians in twos and threes,
Come silently between the trees,
  And wait for me to land.
And if I do not want to play
With any Indians to-day,
  I simply wave my hand.
And then they turn and go away –
  They always understand.

The Second Chair
  I'm a great big lion in my cage,
    And I often frighten Nanny with a roar.
      Then I hold her very tight, and
      Tell her not to be so frightened –
    And she doesn't be so frightened any more.

The Third Chair
> When I am in my ship, I see
> > The other ships go sailing by.
> A sailor leans and calls to me
> > As his tall ship goes sailing by.
> Across the sea he leans to me,
> > Above the wind I hear him cry:
> "Is this the way to Round-the-World?"
> > He calls as he goes by.

The Fourth Chair

Whenever I sit in a high chair
  For breakfast or dinner or tea,
I try to pretend that it's *my* chair,
  And that I am a baby of three.

Shall I go off to South America?
  Shall I put out in my ship to sea?
Or get in my cage and be lions and tigers?
Or – shall I be only Me?

MARKET SQUARE

I had a penny,
A bright new penny,
I took my penny
   To the market square.
I wanted a rabbit,
A little brown rabbit,
And I looked for a rabbit
   'Most everywhere.

For I went to the stall where they sold sweet lavender
("*Only a penny for a bunch of lavender!*").
"Have you got a rabbit, 'cos I don't want lavender?"
   But they hadn't got a rabbit, not anywhere there.

I had a penny,
And I had another penny,
I took my pennies
    To the market square.
I did want a rabbit,
A little baby rabbit,
And I looked for rabbits
    'Most everywhere.

And I went to the stall where they sold fresh mackerel
("*Now then! Tuppence for a fresh-caught mackerel!*").
"Have you got a rabbit, 'cos I don't like mackerel?"
    But they hadn't got a rabbit, not anywhere there.

I found a sixpence,
A little white sixpence.
I took it in my hand
    To the market square.
I was buying my rabbit
(I do like rabbits),
And I looked for my rabbit
    'Most everywhere.

So I went to the stall where they sold fine saucepans
("*Walk up, walk up, sixpence for a saucepan!*").
"Could I have a rabbit, 'cos we've got two saucepans?"
    But they hadn't got a rabbit, not anywhere there.

I had nuffin',
No, I hadn't got nuffin',
So I didn't go down
   To the market square;
But I walked on the common
The old-gold common . . .
And I saw little rabbits
   'Most everywhere!

So I'm sorry for the people who sell fine saucepans,
I'm sorry for the people who sell fresh mackerel,
I'm sorry for the people who sell sweet lavender,
   'Cos they haven't got a rabbit, not anywhere there!

DAFFODOWNDILLY

She wore her yellow sun-bonnet,
  She wore her greenest gown;
She turned to the south wind
  And curtsied up and down.
She turned to the sunlight
  And shook her yellow head,
And whispered to her neighbour:
  "Winter is dead."

WATER-LILIES

Where the water-lilies go
To and fro,
Rocking in the ripples of the water,
Lazy on a leaf lies the Lake King's daughter,
And the faint winds shake her.
Who will come and take her?
I will! I will!
Keep still! Keep still!
Sleeping on a leaf lies the Lake King's daughter . . .
Then the wind comes skipping
To the lilies on the water;
And the kind winds wake her.
Now who will take her?
With a laugh she is slipping
Through the lilies on the water.
Wait! Wait!
Too late, too late!
Only the water-lilies go
To and fro,
Dipping, dipping,
To the ripples of the water.

DISOBEDIENCE

James James
Morrison Morrison
Weatherby George Dupree
Took great
Care of his Mother,
Though he was only three.
James James
Said to his Mother,
"Mother," he said, said he;
"You must never go down to the end of the town,
  if you don't go down with me."

James James
Morrison's Mother
Put on a golden gown,
James James
Morrison's Mother
Drove to the end of the town.
James James
Morrison's Mother
Said to herself, said she:
"I can get right down to the end of the town and be
  back in time for tea."

King John
Put up a notice,
"LOST or STOLEN or STRAYED!
JAMES JAMES
MORRISON'S MOTHER
SEEMS TO HAVE BEEN MISLAID.
LAST SEEN
WANDERING VAGUELY:
QUITE OF HER OWN ACCORD,
SHE TRIED TO GET DOWN TO THE END OF THE
TOWN – **FORTY SHILLINGS REWARD!**"

James James
Morrison Morrison
(Commonly known as Jim)
Told his
Other relations
Not to go blaming *him*.
James James
Said to his Mother,
    "Mother," he said, said he:
"You must *never* go down to the end of the town
    without consulting me."

James James
Morrison's mother
Hasn't been heard of since.
King John
Said he was sorry,
So did the Queen and Prince.
King John
(Somebody told me)
Said to a man he knew:
"If people go down to the end of the town, well,
    what can *anyone do*?"

(*Now then, very softly*)
    J. J.
    M. M.
    W. G. Du P.
    Took great
    C/o his M✻✻✻✻✻
    Though he was only 3.
    J. J.
    Said to his M✻✻✻✻✻
    "M✻✻✻✻✻," he said, said he:
"You-must-never-go-down-to-the-end-of-the-town-
    if-you-don't-go-down-with ME!"

SPRING MORNING

Where am I going? I don't quite know.
Down to the stream where the king-cups grow –
Up to the hill where the pine-trees blow –
Anywhere, anywhere. *I* don't know.

Where am I going? The clouds sail by,
Little ones, baby ones, over the sky.
Where am I going? The shadows pass,
Little ones, baby ones, over the grass.

If you were a cloud, and sailed up there,
You'd sail on water as blue as air,
And you'd see me here in the fields and say:
"Doesn't the sky look green to-day?"

Where am I going? The high rooks call:
"It's awful fun to be born at all."
Where am I going? The ring-doves coo:
"We do have beautiful things to do."

If you were a bird, and lived on high,
You'd lean on the wind when the wind came by,
You'd say to the wind when it took you away:
"*That's* where I wanted to go to-day!"

Where am I going? I don't quite know.
What does it matter where people go?
Down to the wood where the blue-bells grow –
Anywhere, anywhere. *I* don't know.

THE ISLAND

If I had a ship,
I'd sail my ship,
I'd sail my ship
Through Eastern seas;
Down to a beach where the slow waves thunder –
The green curls over and the white falls under –
Boom! Boom! Boom!
On the sun-bright sand.
Then I'd leave my ship and I'd land,
And climb the steep white sand,

And climb to the trees,
The six dark trees,
The coco-nut trees on the cliff's green crown –
Hands and knees
To the coco-nut trees,
Face to the cliff as the stones patter down,
Up, up, up, staggering, stumbling,
Round the corner where the rock is crumbling,
Round this shoulder,
Over this boulder,
Up to the top where the six trees stand. . . .

And there would I rest, and lie,
My chin in my hands, and gaze
At the dazzle of sand below,
And the green waves curling slow,
And the grey-blue distant haze
Where the sea goes up to the sky. . . .

And I'd say to myself as I looked so lazily down at the sea:
"There's nobody else in the world, and the world was made
    for me."

THE THREE FOXES

Once upon a time there were three little foxes
Who didn't wear stockings, and they didn't wear sockses,
But they all had handkerchiefs to blow their noses,
And they kept their handkerchiefs in cardboard boxes.

They lived in the forest in three little houses,
And they didn't wear coats, and they didn't wear trousies.
They ran through the woods on their little bare tootsies,
And they played "Touch last" with a family of mouses.

They didn't go shopping in the High Street shopses,
But caught what they wanted in the woods and copses.
They all went fishing, and they caught three wormses,
They went out hunting, and they caught three wopses.

They went to a Fair, and they all won prizes –
Three plum-puddingses and three mince-pieses.
They rode on elephants and swang on swingses,
And hit three coco-nuts at coco-nut shieses.

That's all that I know of the three little foxes
Who kept their handkerchiefs in cardboard boxes.
They lived in the forest in three little houses,
But they didn't wear coats and they didn't wear trousies.
And they didn't wear stockings and they didn't wear sockses.

POLITENESS

If people ask me,
I always tell them:
"Quite well, thank you, I'm very glad to say."
If people ask me,
I always answer,
"Quite well, thank you, how are you to-day?"
I always answer,
I always tell them,
If they ask me
Politely. . . .
BUT SOMETIMES

I wish

That they wouldn't.

JONATHAN JO

Jonathan Jo
Has a mouth like an "O"
And a wheelbarrow full of surprises;
If you ask for a bat,
Or for something like that,
He has got it, whatever the size is.

If you're wanting a ball,
It's no trouble at all;
Why, the more that you ask for, the merrier –
Like a hoop and a top,
And a watch that won't stop,
And some sweets, and an Aberdeen terrier.

Jonathan Jo
Has a mouth like an "O,"
But this is what makes him so funny
If you give him a smile,
Only once in a while,
Then he never expects any money!

AT THE ZOO

There are lions and roaring tigers, and enormous camels
   and things,
There are biffalo-buffalo-bisons, and a great big bear
   with wings,
There's a sort of a tiny potamus, and a tiny nosserus too –
But *I* gave buns to the elephant when *I* went down to
   the Zoo!

There are badgers and bidgers and bodgers, and a
   Super-in-tendent's House,
There are masses of goats, and a Polar, and different kinds
   of mouse,
And I think there's a sort of a something which is called
   a wallaboo –
But *I* gave buns to the elephant when *I* went down to
   the Zoo!

If you try to talk to the bison, he never quite understands;
You can't shake hands with a mingo – he doesn't like shaking hands.
And lions and roaring tigers *hate* saying, "How do you do?" –
But *I* give buns to the elephant when *I* go down to the Zoo!

RICE PUDDING

What is the matter with Mary Jane?
She's crying with all her might and main,
And she won't eat her dinner – rice pudding again –
What *is* the matter with Mary Jane?

What is the matter with Mary Jane?
I've promised her dolls and a daisy-chain,
And a book about animals – all in vain –
What *is* the matter with Mary Jane?

What is the matter with Mary Jane?
She's perfectly well, and she hasn't a pain;
But, look at her, now she's beginning again! –
What *is* the matter with Mary Jane?

What is the matter with Mary Jane?
I've promised her sweets and a ride in the train,
And I've begged her to stop for a bit and explain –
What *is* the matter with Mary Jane?

What is the matter with Mary Jane?
She's perfectly well and she hasn't a pain,
And it's lovely rice pudding for dinner again! –
What *is* the matter with Mary Jane?

MISSING

Has anybody seen my mouse?

I opened his box for half a minute,
Just to make sure he was really in it,
And while I was looking, he jumped outside!
I tried to catch him, I tried, I tried. . . .
I think he's somewhere about the house.
Has *anyone* seen my mouse?

Uncle John, have you seen my mouse?

Just a small sort of mouse, a dear little brown one,
He came from the country, he wasn't a town one,
So he'll feel all lonely in a London street;
Why, what could he possibly find to eat?

He must be somewhere. I'll ask Aunt Rose:
Have *you* seen a mouse with a woffelly nose?
Oh, somewhere about –
He's just got out . . .

Hasn't *anybody* seen my mouse?

THE KING'S BREAKFAST

The King asked
The Queen, and
The Queen asked
The Dairymaid:
"Could we have some butter for
The Royal slice of bread?"
The Queen asked
The Dairymaid,
The Dairymaid
Said, "Certainly,
I'll go and tell
The cow
Now
Before she goes to bed."

The Dairymaid
She curtsied,

And went and told
The Alderney:
"Don't forget the butter for
The Royal slice of bread."

The Alderney
Said sleepily:
"You'd better tell
His Majesty
That many people nowadays
Like marmalade
Instead."

The Dairymaid
Said, "Fancy!"
And went to
Her Majesty.
She curtsied to the Queen, and
She turned a little red:
"Excuse me,
Your Majesty,
For taking of
The liberty,
But marmalade is tasty, if
It's very
Thickly
Spread."

The Queen said
"Oh!"
And went to
His Majesty:
"Talking of the butter for
The royal slice of bread,
Many people
Think that
Marmalade
Is nicer.
Would you like to try a little
Marmalade
Instead?"

The King said,
"Bother!"
And then he said,
"Oh, deary me!"
The King sobbed, "Oh, deary me!"
And went back to bed.
"Nobody,"
He whimpered,
"Could call me
A fussy man;
I *only* want
A little bit
Of butter for
My bread!"

The Queen said,
"There, there!"
And went to
The Dairymaid.
The Dairymaid
Said, "There, there!"
And went to the shed.
The cow said,
"There, there!
I didn't really
Mean it;
Here's milk for his porringer
And butter for his bread."

The Queen took
The butter
And brought it to
His Majesty;
The King said,
"Butter, eh?"
And bounced out of bed.
"Nobody," he said,
As he kissed her
Tenderly,
"Nobody," he said,
As he slid down
The banisters,
"Nobody,
My darling,
Could call me
A fussy man –
BUT

I do like a little bit of butter to my bread!'

HOPPITY

Christopher Robin goes
Hoppity, hoppity,

Hoppity, hoppity, hop.
Whenever I tell him
Politely to stop it, he
Says he can't possibly stop.

If he stopped hopping, he couldn't go anywhere,
Poor little Christopher
Couldn't go anywhere . . .
That's why he *always* goes
Hoppity, hoppity,
Hoppity,
Hoppity,
Hop.

AT HOME

I want a soldier
(A soldier in a busby),
I want a soldier to come and play with me.
I'd give him cream-cakes
(Big ones, sugar ones),
I'd give him cream-cakes and cream for his tea.

I want a soldier
(A tall one, a red one),
I want a soldier who plays on the drum.
Daddy's going to get one
(He's written to the shopman)
Daddy's going to get one as soon as he can come.

THE WRONG HOUSE

I went into a house, and it wasn't a house,
  It has big steps and a great big hall;
But it hasn't got a garden,
      A garden,
      A garden,
  It isn't like a house at all.

I went into a house, and it wasn't a house,
  It has a big garden and great high wall;
But it hasn't got a may-tree,
      A may-tree,
      A may-tree,
  It isn't like a house at all.

I went into a house and it wasn't a house –
    Slow white petals from the may-tree fall;
But it hasn't got a blackbird,
        A blackbird,
        A blackbird,
    It isn't like a house at all.

I went into a house, and I thought it was a house,
    I could hear from the may-tree the blackbird call. . . .
But nobody listened to it,
        Nobody
        Liked it,
    Nobody wanted it at all.

SUMMER AFTERNOON

Six brown cows walk down to drink
  (*All the little fishes blew bubbles at the may-fly*).
Splash goes the first as he comes to the brink,
  Swish go the tails of the five who follow. . . .
Twelve brown cows bend drinking there
  (*All the little fishes went waggle-tail, waggle-tail*) –
Six from the water and six from the air;
Up and down the river darts a blue-black swallow.

THE DORMOUSE AND THE DOCTOR

There once was a Dormouse who lived in a bed
Of delphiniums (blue) and geraniums (red),
And all the day long he'd a wonderful view
Of geraniums (red) and delphiniums (blue).

A Doctor came hurrying round, and he said:
"Tut-tut, I am sorry to find you in bed.
Just say 'Ninety-nine,' while I look at your chest. . . .
Don't you find that chrysanthemums answer the best?"

The Dormouse looked round at the view and replied
(When he'd said "Ninety-nine") that he'd tried and he'd
    tried,
And much the most answering things that he knew
Were geraniums (red) and delphiniums (blue).

The Doctor stood frowning and shaking his head,
And he took up his shiny silk hat as he said:
"What the patient requires is a change," and he went
To see some chrysanthemum people in Kent.

The Dormouse lay there, and he gazed at the view
Of geraniums (red) and delphiniums (blue),
And he knew there was nothing he wanted instead
Of delphiniums (blue) and geraniums (red).

The Doctor came back and, to show what he meant,
He had brought some chrysanthemum cuttings from Kent.
"Now *these*," he remarked, "give a *much* better view
Than geraniums (red) and delphiniums (blue)."

They took out their spades and they dug up the bed
Of delphiniums (blue) and geraniums (red),
And they planted chrysanthemums (yellow and white).
"And *now*," said the Doctor, "we'll *soon* have you right."

The Dormouse looked out, and he said with a sigh:
"I suppose all these people know better than I.
It was silly, perhaps, but I *did* like the view
Of geraniums (red) and delphiniums (blue)."

The Doctor came round and examined his chest,
And ordered him Nourishment, Tonics, and Rest.
"How very effective," he said, as he shook
The thermometer, "all these chrysanthemums look!"

The Dormouse turned over to shut out the sight
Of the endless chrysanthemums (yellow and white).
"How lovely," he thought, "to be back in a bed
Of delphiniums (blue) and geraniums (red.)"

The Doctor said, "Tut! It's another attack!"
And ordered him Milk and Massage-of-the-back,
And Freedom-from-worry and Drives-in-a-car,
And murmured, "How sweet your chrysanthemums are!"

The Dormouse lay there with his paws to his eyes,
And imagined himself such a pleasant surprise:
"I'll *pretend* the chrysanthemums turn to a bed
Of delphiniums (blue) and geraniums (red)!"

The Doctor next morning was rubbing his hands,
And saying, "There's nobody quite understands
These cases as I do! The cure has begun!
How fresh the chrysanthemums look in the sun!"

The Dormouse lay happy, his eyes were so tight
He could see no chrysanthemums, yellow or white.
And all that he felt at the back of his head
Were delphiniums (blue) and geraniums (red).

And that is the reason (Aunt Emily said)
If a Dormouse gets in a chrysanthemum bed,
You will find (so Aunt Emily says) that he lies
Fast asleep on his front with his paws to his eyes.

SHOES AND STOCKINGS

There's a cavern in the mountain where the old men meet
(*Hammer, hammer, hammer . . .*
Hammer, hammer, hammer . . .)
They make gold slippers for my lady's feet
(*Hammer, hammer, hammer . . .*
Hammer, hammer, hammer . . .)
My lady is marrying her own true knight,
White her gown, and her veil is white,
But she must have slippers on her dainty feet.
Hammer, hammer, hammer . . .
Hammer.

There's a cottage by the river where the old wives meet
(*Chatter, chatter, chatter . . .*
Chatter, chatter, chatter . . .)

They weave gold stockings for my lady's feet
(*Chatter, chatter, chatter . . .*
Chatter, chatter, chatter . . .).
My lady is going to her own true man,
Youth to youth, since the world began,
But she must have stockings on her dainty feet.
Chatter, chatter, chatter . . .
Chatter.

SAND-BETWEEN-THE-TOES

I went down to the shouting sea,
Taking Christopher down with me,
For Nurse had given us sixpence each –
And down we went to the beach.

    We had sand in the eyes and the ears and the nose,
    And sand in the hair, and sand-between-the-toes.
    Whenever a good nor'-wester blows,
    Christopher is certain of
    Sand-between-the-toes.

The sea was galloping grey and white;
Christopher clutched his sixpence tight;
We clambered over the humping sand –
And Christopher held my hand.

    We had sand in the eyes and the ears and the nose,
    And sand in the hair, and sand-between-the-toes.
    Whenever a good nor'-wester blows,
    Christopher is certain of
    Sand-between-the-toes.

There was a roaring in the sky;
The sea-gulls cried as they blew by,
We tried to talk, but had to shout
Nobody else was out.

When we got home, we had sand in the hair,
In the eyes and the ears and everywhere;
Whenever a good nor'-wester blows,
Christopher is found with
Sand-between-the-toes.

KNIGHTS AND LADIES

There is in my old picture book
A page at which I like to look,
Where knights and squires come riding down
The cobbles of some steep old town,
And ladies from beneath the eaves ·
Flutter their bravest handkerchiefs,
Or, smiling proudly, toss down gages . . .
But that was in the Middle Ages.
It wouldn't happen now; but still,
Whenever I look up the hill
Where, dark against the green and blue,
The firs come marching, two by two,
I wonder if perhaps I *might*
See suddenly a shining knight
Winding his way from blue to green –
Exactly as it would have been
Those many, many years ago. . . .

Perhaps I might. You never know.

LITTLE BO-PEEP AND
LITTLE BOY BLUE

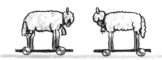

"What have you done with your sheep,
  Little Bo-Peep?
What have you done with your sheep,
  Bo-Peep?"
"Little Boy Blue, what fun!
I've lost them, every one!"
"Oh, what a thing to have done,
  Little Bo-Peep!"

"What have you done with your sheep,
  Little Boy Blue?
What have you done with your sheep,
  Boy Blue?"
"Little Bo-Peep, my sheep
Went off, when I was asleep."
"I'm sorry about your sheep,
  Little Boy Blue."

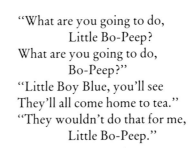

"What are you going to do,
    Little Bo-Peep?
What are you going to do,
    Bo-Peep?"
"Little Boy Blue, you'll see
They'll all come home to tea."
"They wouldn't do that for me,
    Little Bo-Peep."

"What are you going to do,
    Little Boy Blue?
What are you going to do,
    Boy Blue?"
"Little Bo-Peep, I'll blow
My horn for an hour or so."
"Isn't that rather slow,
    Little Boy Blue?"

"Whom are you going to marry,
     Little Bo-Peep?
Whom are you going to marry,
     Bo-Peep?"
"Little Boy Blue, Boy Blue,
I'd like to marry you."
"I think I should like it too,
     Little Bo-Peep."

"Where are we going to live,
     Little Boy Blue?
Where are we going to live,
     Boy Blue?"
"Little Bo-Peep, Bo-Peep,
Up in the hills with the sheep."
"And you'll love your little Bo-Peep,
     Little Boy Blue?"

"I'll love you for ever and ever,
     Little Bo-Peep.
 I'll love you for ever and ever,
     Bo-Peep."
"Little Boy Blue, my dear,
Keep near, keep very near."
"I shall be always here,
     Little Bo-Peep."

THE MIRROR

Between the woods the afternoon
Is fallen in a golden swoon.
The sun looks down from quiet skies
To where a quiet water lies,
    And silent trees stoop down to trees.
And there I saw a white swan make
Another white swan in the lake;
And, breast to breast, both motionless,
They waited for the wind's caress . . .
    And all the water was at ease.

HALFWAY DOWN

Halfway down the stairs
Is a stair
Where I sit.
There isn't any
Other stair
Quite like
It.
I'm not at the bottom,
I'm not at the top;
So this is the stair
Where
I always
Stop.

Halfway up the stairs
Isn't up,
And isn't down.
It isn't in the nursery,
It isn't in the town.
And all sorts of funny thoughts
Run round my head:
"It isn't really
Anywhere!
It's somewhere else
Instead!"

THE INVADERS

In careless patches through the wood
The clumps of yellow primrose stood,
And sheets of white anemones,
Like driven snow against the trees,
Had covered up the violet,
But left the blue-bell bluer yet.

Along the narrow carpet ride,
With primroses on either side,
Between their shadows and the sun,
The cows came slowly, one by one,
Breathing the early morning air
And leaving it still sweeter there.
And, one by one, intent upon
Their purposes, they followed on
In ordered silence . . . and were gone

But all the little wood was still,
As if it waited so, until
Some blackbird on an outpost yew,
Watching the slow procession through,
Lifted his yellow beak at last
To whistle that the line had passed. . . .
Then all the wood began to sing
Its morning anthem to the spring.

BEFORE TEA

Emmeline
Has not been seen
For more than a week. She slipped between
The two tall trees at the end of the green . . .
We all went after her. "*Emmeline!*"

"Emmeline,
I didn't mean –
I only said that your hands weren't clean."
We went to the trees at the end of the green . . .
But Emmeline
Was not to be seen.

Emmeline
Came slipping between
The two tall trees at the end of the green.
We all ran up to her. "Emmeline!
Where have you been?
Where have you been?
Why, it's more than a week!" And Emmeline
Said, "Sillies, I went and saw the Queen.
She says my hands are *purfickly* clean!"

TEDDY BEAR

A bear, however hard he tries,
Grows tubby without exercise.
Our Teddy Bear is short and fat,
Which is not to be wondered at;
He gets what exercise he can
By falling off the ottoman,
But generally seems to lack
The energy to clamber back.

Now tubbiness is just the thing
Which gets a fellow wondering;
And Teddy worried lots about
The fact that he was rather stout.
He thought: "If only I were thin!
But how does anyone begin?"
He thought: "It really isn't fair
To grudge me exercise and air."

For many weeks he pressed in vain
His nose against the window-pane,
And envied those who walked about
Reducing their unwanted stout.
None of the people he could see
"Is quite" (he said) "as fat as me!"
Then, with a still more moving sigh,
"I mean" (he said) "as fat as I!"

Now Teddy, as was only right,
Slept in the ottoman at night,
And with him crowded in as well
More animals than I can tell;
Not only these, but books and things,
Such as a kind relation brings –
Old tales of "Once upon a time,"
And history retold in rhyme.

One night it happened that he took
A peep at an old picture-book,
Wherein he came across by chance
The picture of a King of France
(A stoutish man) and, down below,
These words: "King Louis So and So,
Nicknamed 'The Handsome!'" There he sat,
And (think of it!) the man was fat!

Our bear rejoiced like anything
To read about this famous King,
Nicknamed "The Handsome." There he sat,
And certainly the man was fat.
Nicknamed "The Handsome." Not a doubt
The man was definitely stout.
Why then, a bear (for all his tub)
Might yet be named "The Handsome Cub!"

"Might yet be named." Or did he mean
That years ago he "might have been"?
For now he felt a slight misgiving:
"Is Louis So and So still living?
Fashions in beauty have a way
Of altering from day to day.
Is 'Handsome Louis' with us yet?
Unfortunately I forget."

Next morning (nose to window-pane)
The doubt occurred to him again.
One question hammered in his head:
"Is he alive or is he dead?"
Thus, nose to pane, he pondered; but
The lattice window, loosely shut,
Swung open. With one startled "Oh!"
Our Teddy disappeared below.

There happened to be passing by
A plump man with a twinkling eye,
Who, seeing Teddy in the street,
Raised him politely to his feet,
And murmured kindly in his ear
Soft words of comfort and of cheer:
"Well, well!" "Allow me!" "Not at all."
"Tut-tut! A very nasty fall."

Our Teddy answered not a word;
It's doubtful if he even heard.
Our bear could only look and look:
The stout man in the picture-book!
That "handsome" King – could this be he,
This man of adiposity?
"Impossible," he thought. "But still,
No harm in asking. Yes I will!"

"Are you," he said, "by any chance
His Majesty the King of France?"
The other answered, "I am that,"
Bowed stiffly, and removed his hat;
Then said, "Excuse me," with an air,
"But is it Mr Edward Bear?"
And Teddy, bending very low,
Replied politely, "Even so!"

They stood beneath the window there,
The King and Mr Edward Bear,
And, handsome, if a trifle fat,
Talked carelessly of this and that . . .
Then said His Majesty, "Well, well,
I must get on," and rang the bell.
"Your bear, I think," he smiled. "Good-day!"
And turned, and went upon his way.

A bear, however hard he tries,
Grows tubby without exercise.
Our Teddy Bear is short and fat,
Which is not to be wondered at.
But do you think it worries him
To know that he is far from slim?
No, just the other way about –
He's *proud* of being short and stout.

BAD SIR BRIAN BOTANY

Sir Brian had a battleaxe with great big knobs on;
  He went among the villagers and blipped them on the
    head.
On Wednesday and on Saturday, but mostly on the latter
    day,
  He called at all the cottages, and this is what he said:
      "I am Sir Brian!" (*ting-ling*)
        "I am Sir Brian!" (*rat-tat*)
      "I am Sir Brian, as bold as a lion –
        Take *that!* – and *that!* – and *that!*"

Sir Brian had a pair of boots with great big spurs on,
  A fighting pair of which he was particularly fond.
On Tuesday and on Friday, just to make the street look tidy,
  He'd collect the passing villagers and kick them in the
    pond.
      "I am Sir Brian!" (*sper-lash!*)
        "I am Sir Brian!" (*sper-losh!*)
      "I am Sir Brian, as bold as a lion –
        Is anyone else for a wash?"

Sir Brian woke one morning, and he couldn't find his
    battleaxe;
  He walked into the village in his second pair of boots.
He had gone a hundred paces, when the street was full of
    faces,
  And the villagers were round him with ironical salutes.
    "You are Sir Brian? Indeed!
      You are Sir Brian? Dear, dear!
    You are Sir Brian, as bold as a lion?
      Delighted to meet you here!"

Sir Brian went on a journey, and he found a lot of duckweed:

  They pulled him out and dried him, and they blipped him
    on the head.
They took him by the breeches, and they hurled him into
    ditches,
  And they pushed him under waterfalls, and this is what
    they said:

"You are Sir Brian – don't laugh,
  You are Sir Brian – don't cry;
You are Sir Brian, as bold as a lion –
  Sir Brian, the lion, good-bye!"

Sir Brian struggled home again, and chopped up his battleaxe,
  Sir Brian took his fighting boots, and threw them in the
    fire.
He is quite a different person now he hasn't got his spurs on,
  And he goes about the village as B. Botany, Esquire.
    "I am Sir Brian? Oh, *no!*
      I am Sir Brian? Who's he?
    I haven't got any title, I'm Botany –
      Plain Mr Botany (B)."

IN THE FASHION

A lion has a tail and a very fine tail,
And so has an elephant, and so has a whale,
And so has a crocodile, and so has a quail –
    They've all got tails but me.

If I had sixpence I would buy one;
I'd say to the shopman, "Let me try one;"
I'd say to the elephant, "This is *my* one."
    They'd all come round to see.

Then I'd say to the lion, "Why, *you've* got a tail!
And so has the elephant, and so has the whale!
And, look! There's a crocodile! *He's* got a tail!
    You've all got tails like me!"

THE ALCHEMIST

There lives an old man at the top of the street,
And the end of his beard reaches down to his feet,
And he's just the one person I'm longing to meet,
   I think that he sounds so exciting;
For he talks all the day to his tortoiseshell cat,
And he asks about this, and explains about that,
And at night he puts on a big wide-awake* hat
   And sits in the writing-room, writing.

He has worked all his life (and he's terribly old)
At a wonderful spell which says, "Lo and behold!
Your nursery fender is gold!" – and it's gold!
   (Or the tongs, or the rod for the curtain);
But somehow he hasn't got hold of it quite,
Or the liquid you pour on it first isn't right,
So that's why he works at it night after night
   Till he knows he can do it for certain.

*So as not to go to sleep.

GROWING UP

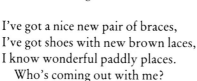

I've got shoes with grown-up laces,
I've got knickers and a pair of braces,
I'm all ready to run some races.
  Who's coming out with me?

I've got a nice new pair of braces,
I've got shoes with new brown laces,
I know wonderful paddly places.
  Who's coming out with me?

Every morning my new grace is,
"Thank you, God, for my nice braces;
I can tie my new brown laces."
  Who's coming out with me?

IF I WERE KING

I often wish I were a King,
And then I could do anything.

If only I were King of Spain,
I'd take my hat off in the rain.

If only I were King of France,
I wouldn't brush my hair for aunts.

I think, if I were King of Greece,
I'd push things off the mantelpiece.

If I were King of Norroway,
I'd ask an elephant to stay.

If I were King of Babylon,
I'd leave my button gloves undone.

If I were King of Timbuctoo,
I'd think of lovely things to do.

If I were King of anything,
I'd tell the soldiers, "I'm the King!"

VESPERS

Little Boy kneels at the foot of the bed,
Droops on the little hands little gold head.
Hush! Hush! Whisper who dares!
Christopher Robin is saying his prayers.

God bless Mummy. I know that's right.
Wasn't it fun in the bath to-night?
The cold's so cold, and the hot's so hot.
Oh! *God bless Daddy* – I quite forgot.

If I open my fingers a little bit more,
I can see Nanny's dressing-gown on the door.
It's a beautiful blue, but it hasn't a hood.
Oh! *God bless Nanny and make her good.*

Mine has a hood, and I lie in bed,
And pull the hood right over my head,
And I shut my eyes, and I curl up small,
And nobody knows that I'm there at all.

Oh! *Thank you, God, for a lovely day.*
And what was the other I had to say?
I said "Bless Daddy," so what can it be?
Oh! Now I remember it. *God bless Me.*

Little Boy kneels at the foot of the bed,
Droops on the little hands little gold head.
Hush! Hush! Whisper who dares!
Christopher Robin is saying his prayers.